A Time for

BABIES

A Time for
BABIES

Ron Hirschi

PHOTOGRAPHS BY Thomas D. Mangelsen

A HOW ANIMALS LIVE Book

COBBLEHILL BOOKS/Dutton
New York

For Jordan.
—R.H.

For Mary.
—T.M.

Library of Congress Cataloging-in-Publication Data
Hirschi, Ron.
        A time for babies / Ron Hirschi ; photographs by Thomas D.
Mangelsen.
        p.   cm. —(A How animals live book)
        Summary: Text and photographs depict the raising of their young
by various animals, including the grizzly bear, eagle, and fox.
        ISBN 0-525-65095-4
        1. Animals—Infancy—Juvenile literature.   [1. Animals—Infancy.]
I. Mangelsen, Thomas D., ill.   II. Title.   III. Series.
QL763.H57   1993
591.3'9—dc20   92-21409   CIP   AC

Published in the United States by Cobblehill Books,
an affiliate of Dutton Children's Books, a division of
Penguin Books USA Inc., 375 Hudson Street, New York, New York 10014
Designed by Charlotte Staub
Printed in Hong Kong
First edition 10 9 8 7 6 5 4 3 2 1

Mother polar bear and cub

On the coldest snowy nights—
even when winter winds still howl—
it is time for babies to be born.
Long before the flowers of spring,
polar bear cubs are born in their mother's den.

The baby bears grow fast on mother's rich milk.
They soon search outside for a place to play
or snuggle with brother or sister.

Grizzly bear cubs are born in winter too.
When wildflowers bloom, they

Grizzly bear and cubs

Grizzly bears fishing

follow mom to the riverbank.
Leaping fish jump the rapids
and the bears must be quick
to catch a fresh fish
breakfast.

Baby owls, all covered with downy feathers, are among the first birds to be born in spring.

Their parents keep a watchful eye for predators.

Great horned owls

Bald eagles

Eaglets are born
in spring too.

The eagle parents

fly swift and strong to catch food
for their nestlings.

Bald eagles

Peregrine falcon

Rare birds of great beauty, falcons
often raise their babies

Peregrine falcon

in cliffside nests near the sea.
The falcons hunt seabirds
out over the ocean waves

Peregrine falcons

Atlantic puffin

where puffins catch
mouthfuls of slender
silver fish to feed
babies of their own.

Arctic terns and chick

Baby terns beg
fish from their
parents too.

Common mergansers

Mother merganser teaches her babies to
catch fish on their own.

The merganser ducklings ride on mom's back
or rest on the riverbank after a
swim in the swift current.

Common mergansers

A sandhill crane pecks at the egg while its parent stands nearby.

Sandhill crane at nest

Sandhill crane hatching

The chick struggles to break free of its protective shell.

Sandhill crane

Then the baby sandhill hatches,
drying its feathers in the sun,
and walking its first steps in
the late spring wildflowers.

Canada geese

Baby loons and baby geese swim soon after

Common loons

they break free from their eggshells.

Red foxes

Baby foxes play or sleep outside their den in the warm sun.

But baby warblers and baby hummingbirds
are too tiny to walk, too tiny to run,
and too helpless to fly.
The nestlings are almost naked at birth
and must be kept warm and sheltered
from spring rain and cold winds.
But in three short weeks they will fly.
In three short months they will travel
all the way to Mexico and beyond.

Yellow warblers

Broad-tailed hummingbirds

Elk calves play-fighting

Elk calves run and
jump soon after birth.
Their long legs are wobbly
but strong like the
deer fawn.

The spotted fawn
follows its mother,
learns where to hide,
grows each day, and
plays a lot too.

Mule deer

Mountain bluebirds

Bluebird babies need
a place to be born you
could make for them.
Then the bluebird parents
can lay their eggs.
There will always be
more babies if you lend a
helping hand when time for
babies comes next year.

Afterword

No time of the year is more critical for wildlife survival than the time for babies. And, this time of birth does not just happen in spring. In fact, birth comes at varying times, even for the same animal— bluebirds, for example, can have their babies any time from March to July. The time of egg laying for these and other birds can vary, depending on weather extremes and on food availability.

Owls and eagles usually have their little ones before any other birds. Their eggs can be in the nest by February and the young hatch when mice and other prey are abundant. Bears are early too—young are born in winter dens where they nurse until spring. The enormous polar bear can weigh as much as 1,500 pounds as an adult, but its cubs weigh as little as one pound at birth. Amazingly, these tiny bears are born at the coldest time of the year.

No matter when young animals are born, the critical needs they have for survival are almost completely in our hands. We must protect their nesting and denning areas. And large natural habitats are needed for feeding, first flights, and for new places for another generation to be born in coming years.